Chambers
gigglossary
a lexicon of laughter

Something to make you laugh.
all the way from my
hometown Ottawa!

Love ya

Susan

Chambers

CHAMBERS
An imprint of Chambers Harrap Publishers Ltd
7 Hopetoun Crescent, Edinburgh, EH7 4AY

First published by Chambers Harrap Publishers Ltd 2008

Text copyright © Chambers Harrap Publishers Ltd 2008

Illustrations copyright © Iain McIntosh 2008

A CIP catalogue record for this book is available from the British Library.

ISBN 978 0550 10414 4

Editors: Vicky Aldus, Morven Dooner
Editorial Assistance: Kathleen Sargeant
Introduction by Dr Julie Coleman with extra material from
Chambers Gigglossary booklet 2006
Additional material: Roddy Lumsden
Prepress Controller: Andrew Butterworth

Designed and typeset by Chambers Harrap Publishers Ltd, Edinburgh
Typeset in Miller Text
Printed and bound by Clays Ltd, St Ives plc

CONTENTS

see accountant, *page 82*

see Poodle

page 117

ACKNOWLEDGEMENTS

The editors would like to thank everyone who has contributed to our online Gigglossary project, in particular the following contributors, whose witty definitions appear in this book

Roy Adams
Ant Allan
Mike Allen
Peter Allen
Warwick Annear
Carol Baxter
Kevin Boddington
Peter Bones
Jo Buckingham
Gordon Burnside
Chris Butler
David Canning
Dick Chinnery
Andy Cole
J A Coleman
David Cook
S Cotechini
N S Cowley
Henry Drury
Nigel Drury
Ian Duffy
Alan J K Duval
Simon Fowles
P Gheorghiu
Patrick Griffin
Marcus Han
Ross Hay
David Hedges

Madison Higgs
Robert Hirst
Patrick Hoyte
Leo Huckvale
Robert James
N Jones
Neil Jones
Terry John
G Kelly
Ned Kelly
Ambrose Kennedy
Warren Keyes
Tim King
John Lamper
B H Langleben
Iain Leonard
Pierre Leroux
Trevor Livings
Keith Lord
Rick Luskin
B Macauley
R McCarthy
Brian McIntyre
Elisabeth McOwan
Ignacio Mancini
Priscilla Mann
Richard May
Lawrence Mayes

Vincent Murray
Joe O'Farrell
Ben Paddon
Dave Peters
Billy Price
Dave Pugh
Tobias Reynolds
T Ridd
F E Rose
David Rowe
R Saunders
Chris Simmons
Shankar Sivanandan
A Smith
Peter M Smith
Phil Smith
Jeff Sparkes
Simon Stacey
Sam Thewlis
J T B Visser
Damien Whinnery
Ledger White
N Wong
Chris Wyles
Steve Wylie
Yamraaj

WHAT IS A GIGGLOSSARY?

The lexicographer was defined by Samuel Johnson as 'a writer of dictionaries; a harmless drudge, that busies himself in tracing the original, and detailing the signification of words.'

This may be true, but there has long been a tradition of these harmless drudges injecting the occasional humorous definition into the weighty content of the English dictionary. This practice was started by none other than the formidable Dr Johnson himself in his *Dictionary of the English Language* of 1755.

Ever since its first edition in 1901, *The Chambers Dictionary* has upheld this tradition by including a smattering of witty entries, the most celebrated of which is probably that of *éclair*: 'a cake, long in shape but short in duration, with cream filling and usually chocolate icing.'

Since 2003, many visitors to the Chambers website (www.chambers.co.uk) have joined in the fun by contributing their own funny definitions to our online *Gigglossary*.

Within these pages you will find a whole alphabetful of amusing definitions, including our favourites from *The Chambers Dictionary*; notable and quotable definitions by famous wits; and a wealth of new funnies written by contributors to the *Gigglossary* and by Chambers lexicographers.

DEFINITIONS OF HUMOUR

humour or *US* **humor**
a mental quality that apprehends and delights in the ludicrous and mirthful; that which causes mirth and amusement; the quality of being funny; playful fancy

In response to the revelation that I spend my time working on dictionaries, a tax adviser (of all people!) said 'That sounds boring'. Dictionaries and humour clearly seem an unpromising pairing. What can there possibly be to say? Well, an Amazon search for *dictionary* and *humour* produces over 300 results. There are humorous dictionaries of golf, snooker, fishing, computing, football, left-handedness, dating, sex and rats (really), as well as various dialects and registers of English. Browse through the books in the humour section of a bookshop and you will invariably find a comic glossary of some description.

The reason that dictionaries can be funny is that they are usually seen to be so utterly lacking in humour. There are clear rules about what can and what can't be said in a dictionary, as well as rules about how it's supposed to be said. Playing with these expectations can cause a surprised snort, but it also pokes fun at the perceived idea of the pompous know-all who writes serious dictionaries.

Perhaps it's useful to start with a description of what we expect when we pick up a dictionary. We expect an alphabetical arrangement of words (known in the business as *headwords* or *lemmata*) with explanations of their meanings (*definitions*) and some information about how they're used. Some dictionaries include information about the word's origins (its *etymology*) or a guide to how it's pronounced. There are often cross-references pointing us to related words. Some offer examples to show the words in use, and some provide diagrams to make the meanings of words clearer still.

Above all, we expect dictionaries to be impersonal, objective and concise. Many of us consult a dictionary when we need advice on which words to use, but we don't expect dictionaries to tell us how to think.

Such a detailed set of expectations leaves plenty of scope for playing around with the dictionary format and in this little book we hope to introduce you to some of the different types of humour to be found in the humble dictionary – hopefully doing so without jokeicidal over-analysis.

'The dictionary' hasn't always had a well-established format to follow, and this means that some of the oldest dictionaries sometimes seem humorous to us when they probably didn't seem so at the time they were written. When he published his groundbreaking *Dictionary of the English Language* in 1755, Samuel Johnson was establishing a new standard by trying to include all the commonly used words in English as

Dr. Johnson

well as the difficult ones from Latin and Greek. The problem is that common words can be very hard to define. If you understand 'a convulsion of the lungs, vellicated by some sharp serosity', you probably don't need to look up *cough*, for example. 'Any thing reticulated or decussated, at equal distances, with interstices between the intersections' may indeed

3

describe a *network*, but it doesn't make the word any easier to understand. Nathan Bailey's *Universal Etymological English Dictionary* of 1721 included the following at the opposite extreme of this particular type of dictionary humour:

> **mouse** an animal well-known

Humorous or barbed comments tucked away in an otherwise serious alphabetical listing can provide a glimpse of the personality behind the apparently objective tone of the dictionary. Johnson's blatantly opinionated definitions give us a fascinating insight into his character:

> **fishing** a stick and a string, with a worm at one end and a fool at the other

When he penned the following definition:

> **patron** commonly a wretch who supports with insolence, and is paid with flattery

he knew that informed readers would see this as a reference to his own dealings with the Earl of Chesterfield (who tried to take credit for Johnson's dictionary without providing the financial support its author badly needed during his nine years' work).

Some of Johnson's most famous definitions and examples were uncharacteristically humble:

> **dull** to make dictionaries is dull work

> **lexicographer** a harmless drudge

Perhaps because of this last point, dictionary-makers from Johnson to the present day can be excused for attempting to lighten their days by lacing the sober bulk of their work with the occasional witty definition, although most serious dictionaries would probably insist on a less subjective tone.

Johnson is quite justly the most famous early proponent of the humorous definition, but he was by no means alone. It is when we look at his less well-known contemporaries that we realise just how timeless Johnson's ingenious and pithy definitions are. These examples of eighteenth-century wit in dictionaries have not stood the test of time quite so successfully. From Francis Grose's *Classical Dictionary of the Vulgar Tongue* (1785):

> **Cods** nick name for a curate. A rude fellow meeting a curate, mistook him for a rector; and accosted him with the vulgar appellation of Bol—ks the rector, 'No Sir,' answered he, 'only Cods the curate, at your service.'

> **public ledger** a prostitute: because, like that paper, she is open to all parties.

> **whore-monger** a man that keeps more than one mistress. A country gentlemen, who kept a female friend, being reproved by the parson of the parish, and styled a whore-monger, asked the parson whether he had a cheese in his house; and being answered in the affirmative, 'Pray,' says he, 'does that one cheese make you a cheese-monger?'

In the earliest known dictionary of college slang, *Gradus ad Cantabrigiam* (1803), many of the entries provide an undergraduate's view of university regulations:

ægrotat permission to be absent from chapel and lecture, on account of corporal indisposition – though, commonly, the real complaint is much more serious; viz. *indisposition of the mind*!

dormiat to take out a dormiat. *Phr.* a license to sleep. The licensed person is excused from attending early prayers in the Chapel, from a plea of being really *indisposed* – ie to attend!

– which perhaps goes to prove that even if humour has changed over the centuries, the stereotypical student has not!

The Chambers Dictionary is unique among contemporary mainstream dictionaries in including humorous definitions scattered among its more serious ones. From the very first edition in 1901, *Chambers's Twentieth Century Dictionary* (as it was then known) included  definitions which were without doubt of a witty bent, for example:

charity begins at home usually an excuse for not allowing it to get abroad

sea serpent an enormous marine animal of serpent-like form, frequently seen and described by credulous sailors, imaginative landsmen and common liars

This idiosyncratic approach became regarded as a Chambers hallmark, and later editors built on the tradition, including further light-hearted entries in subsequent editions:

buckwheat a plant (*Polygonum* or *Fagopyrum*), its seed used especially in Europe for feeding horses, cattle and poultry, in America for making into cakes for the breakfast table, etc

1952 edition

éclair a cake, long in shape but short in duration, with cream filling and usually chocolate icing

1952 edition

flag day a day on which collectors solicit contributions to a charity in exchange for small flags as badges to secure immunity for the rest of the day

supplement to 1901 edition (1933)

middle age between youth and old age, variously reckoned to suit the reckoner

1952 edition

The definition of *buckwheat* is undoubtedly a nod towards Johnson's *oat* 'a grain, which in England is generally given to horses, but in Scotland supports the people.'

In 1972 it was decided that these definitions had no place in a serious reference work, and many were edited out. This cull was met by howls of disapproval from devoted users who had, presumably, traded up to a new edition and immediately checked that their favourites were still there. The funnies were restored in 1983 and have been added to ever since:

man-eater a woman given to chasing, catching, and devouring men

1988 edition

tracksuit a loose warm suit intended to be worn by athletes when warming up or training, but sometimes worn by others in an error of judgement

2003 edition

A hidden treat in a film, DVD, CD or computer game is known as an *easter egg*, and perhaps this term could be stretched to include *The Chambers Dictionary*'s humorous definitions.

The popularity of Chambers' humorous definitions gave rise to *Chambers Gigglossary*, the online project which provided part of the inspiration for this book. Visitors to the Chambers website (www.chambers.co.uk) are invited to submit their own humorous definitions, the best of which are posted on the site. Many follow the Chambers format of commenting on the accepted use of normal terms:

confidence the feeling one experiences before one fully understands the situation

R. McCarthy

naturist a person who prefers to go about naked, and by doing so reminds others why it's such a good idea to go about clothed

R. James

unbelievable a word used by sports commentators to describe any normal event

G. Kelly

You will find hundreds of witty definitions from *The Chambers Dictionary*, and from the online *Chambers Gigglossary* later in this book.

Sometimes it is not quite clear whether the lexicographer was aiming to create a comic effect or not. Was the editor of *The Chambers Dictionary* who defined *abloom* as 'in a blooming state' aware of the ambiguity involved? Similarly, one wonders whether the person who defined the wood-eating *Xylophaga* as 'a genus of boring bivalves' was deliberately trying to be funny.

Other dictionaries contain definitions which are unintentionally funny, and the determinedly puerile will find much amusement in the *Oxford English Dictionary* with entries such as:

associate to keep company or have intercourse (with)

bellhouse a tower or other erection for containing a bell or set of bells ...

interjaculate to ejaculate in the midst of a conversation ...

Of course these gleams of gold in the gritty matter of serious dictionaries are a small part of the humour to be found in defining. The humorous dictionary was an inevitable product of the comic potential of the dictionary format.

Ambrose Bierce was an American journalist and satirist who included satirical definitions in his newspaper columns. These were later collected as *The Cynic's Wordbook* in 1906, and re-published with his preferred title, *The Devil's Dictionary*, in 1911. It is perhaps the best-known example of a comic dictionary: a book that subverts the dictionary format for comic effect. Bierce used his definitions to comment on various aspects of contemporary life:

clarionet an instrument of torture operated by a person with cotton in his ears. There are two instruments worse than a clarionet – two clarionets

learning the kind of ignorance distinguishing the studious

referendum a law for submission of proposed legislation to a popular vote to learn the nonsensus of public opinion

see bellhouse

> **year** a period of three hundred and sixty-five disappointments

The format was reproduced in many subsequent books, including Evan Esar's *Comic Dictionary* of 1943:

> **play** work that you enjoy doing for nothing

> **statistics** the only science that enables different experts using the same figures to draw different conclusions

From *Alphabet Soup* (1997), a collection of aphorisms by poet and satirist Leslie Woolf Hedley:

> **advice** make certain you have rich parents

> **chess** boredom made complicated

Humour isn't just for light-hearted entertainment, though. It can be used to avoid confronting unpleasant realities, and many dictionaries of the slang of soldiers serving in the two World Wars favour misdefinition as a way of making light of inhuman conditions and incompetent or incomprehensible bureaucracy. These examples are from 'Tommy's Dictionary of the Trenches', an American's account of British trench language in Arthur Guy Empey's *Over the Top* (1917):

> **adjutant** the name given to an officer who helps the Colonel do nothing. He rides a horse and you see him at guard mounting and battalion parade.

11

> **iron rations** a tin of bully beef, two biscuits, and a tin containing tea, sugar, and Oxo cubes. These are not supposed to be eaten until you die of starvation.

> **rifle** part of Tommy's armament. Its main use is to be cleaned. Sometimes it is fired, when you are not using a pick or shovel.

First World War comic definitions often emphasise the distance between the troops' and their officers' understanding of the experience of war. This type of comic glossary is found in several informal and unofficial 'troop journals', published by the troops for the troops in or near the front line. Other examples imply that language is deliberately misused in an attempt to fool the troops into believing that conditions were better than they were:

> **bacon** a mythical breakfast dish rumoured to have been issued to soldiers sometime in the forgotten past ...
>
> 'The Dictionary of War Terms', *The Listening Post*

> **leave** a fictitious period of leisure supposed to be spent in Blighty
>
> *Golden Horseshoe*

Another technique was to emphasize the differences between civilian expectations and military reality:

> **Flanders** a piece of mud almost surrounded by water
>
> 'Definitions in memory of H.M.F.', *The Dump*

> **rain** a liquid. One of the main ingredients used in the process of making mud. Also used to find the holes in tents.
>
> 'Dictionary of War Terms', *The Sting*

> **trench** a long narrow excavation in earth or chalk, sometimes filled with mud containing soldiers, bits of soldiers, salvage and alleged shelters
>
> *Aussie Dictionary*

Dictionaries of Second World War slang also used humour, but in very different ways to the glossaries of First World War slang. Often upbeat and considerably less cynical, they were designed to raise morale rather than to record the soldiers' emotions. The introductions tended to be written by senior officers emphasizing what fun it was to be in the army. Johnny Viney's *Hi Hattie* (1941) includes:

> **AOL** absent over leave. Probably delayed by a brunette, tch tch. Or a blonde, tch tch tch. Or a red head, tch tch tch. That's terrible. By the way, what's her phone number?

> **fresh water wrench** fun to send a recruit after

> **navy cocktail** castor oil gaulluppgullup-gulluup UGH!

An online humorous dictionary of computer terms brings the concept of misdefinition of genuine words bang up to date:

> **keyboard** the standard way to generate computer errors

obsolete any computer you own

state-of-the-art any computer you can't afford

Park Kendall's 'Army Slang' glossary in *Still in the Draft* uses excessively elaborate language to explain refusals and rejections:

Horsecollar, Soldiers! I do not wish to question the sincerity of your statement but might I suggest that you re-check the sources of information on which your affirmation is predicated.

see the Chaplain! I greatly regret that there is nothing I can do to assist you. ... Being a gentleman, I hesitate to tell you to shut your face. So may I suggest that you see the Chaplain.

Humorous dialect dictionaries play with language in the same way, for instance, Frank Shaw's *Lern Yerself Scouse* (1966) includes:

yer a dirty stopout you are a nocturnal reveller

she gave im de rounds uv de kitchen they had a domestic altercation

In both these dictionaries, the humour lies in the impossibility of comprehension between the standard and the non-standard speaker of English. They suggest a pompous lexicographer struggling to define the intricacies of the life of the 'ordinary' person.

Afferbeck Lauder's *Let Stalk Strine*, published in 1965, took Australian English as its target, and was one of the first comic dictionaries to look at non-standard forms of English. It drew attention to Australian pronunciation, and its tendency to run words together:

> **egg jelly** in fact; really. As in: 'Well there's nothing really egg jelly the matter with her.'

> **Sander's lape** in a state of suspended animation. As in: 'Doan mica noise, Norm, the kiddies are Sander's lape.'

Misunderstandings can easily come out of national and regional differences in use, and an early American slang dictionary, Eruera Tooné's *Yankee Slang* (1932), often comments on these:

> **honey** a friendly greeting. 'Say Honey, what's eatin' you?' 'Bring me some water, Honey.' In a London restaurant I asked a waitress 'Fetch me coffee and sandwiches, Honey.' Coffee, sandwiches, and a pot of honey duly appeared!

The conversational tone seen here is echoed in John Blackman's *Aussie Slang Dictionary* where the author's gags play an important part in his definitions, defying the dictionary convention of brief and impersonal definitions:

> **bag** uncomplimentary term for a woman. Wives are sometimes referred to as 'the old bag' (except mine of course!).

> **mollydooker** a left-hander. Personally, I'd give my right hand to be ambidextrous!

The Internet has brought the dictionary format into the 21st century's virtual world, and online, user-edited dictionaries provide scope for a more partial, informal style, and a much more aggressive type of humour. Gone completely are the carefully worded, finely crafted definitions; the personal opinions of each contributor are clearly and unashamedly displayed. From *The Urban Dictionary* (www.urban dictionary.com):

chav a human sub-species also known as homo-inferior. They plan to conquer the world by lowering the nation's IQ to single digit numbers…

feminist a strong advocate of women's rights and equality… Until the check [bill] comes…

Humorous definitions are of course not limited to the world of dictionaries: artists, playwrights, intellectuals, satirists and wits through the ages have delighted us with clever and memorable definitions, many of which have become so ubiquitous that no one is really sure who came up with them first. Oscar Wilde was one of the most prolific creators of quotable definitions, which were sprinkled liberally into his conversation as well as his writings. He is commonly credited with:

Bigamy is having one wife too many. Monogamy is the same.

> Extravagance is the luxury of the poor; penury is the luxury of the rich.

and he can certainly take credit for:

> A cynic is a man who knows the price of everything, and the value of nothing.
>
> *Lady Windermere's Fan*

Although he is now arguably best known for *Tom Sawyer* and *Huckleberry Finn*, Mark Twain was an incisive satirist, and is credited with:

> Climate is what we expect, weather is what we get.

> Wit is the sudden marriage of ideas which before their union were not perceived to have any relation.

He certainly did write:

> Cauliflower is nothing but cabbage with a college education.
>
> *Pudd'nhead Wilson*

In a rather more sombre tone, Woody Allen is credited with:

> Marriage is the death of hope.

> Tradition is the illusion of permanence.

This type of aphorism is quoted so frequently that it can be transformed by misquotation. Whether these witty one-liners began as definitions or were transformed into them over the years, they do show that the dictionary format is a useful shorthand for a seriousness that is quickly undercut by the subversive definition.

So much for humorous definitions of real words. Another type of dictionary-based humour relies on the provision of definitions for words and phrases that don't exist at all. An online 'dictionary of non-existent words', by Matthew Feinberg, called the *Nonsensicon* lists:

quiggiligus one of the individual holes in the mesh on most speakers

ziqx a word with no meaning designed only for use in Scrabble®

Many other entries in the *Nonsensicon* are blends, where two real words are combined to produce a new form. Some words built in this way do endure, like brunch (from *breakfast* and *lunch*) or motel (from *motor* and *hotel*). Judge for yourself whether you think the following might catch on:

frisbeterian someone who religiously spends Sunday afternoons teaching his/her dog to catch a Frisbee®

unobtainium the perfect material for the job, which does not exist, or cannot be had

In 1983 Douglas Adams and John Lloyd enjoyed phenomenal success with *The Meaning of Liff*, a book which listed intriguing sounding place-names and gave them outlandish definitions. These were often based on the sound of the word or a concept which struck a chord with readers but for which no English word existed. Thus *Nempnett Thrubwell* was defined as 'the feeling experienced when driving off for the very first time on a brand new motorbike', *Trunch* as 'the instinctive resentment of people younger than you,' and *Yarmouth* as 'to shout at foreigners in the belief that the louder you speak, the better they'll understand you.'

Inventing words in order to define them was a device frequently employed by opponents of political correctness, often in television comedies such as *The Two Ronnies* (where *personhole* and *Personchester* were suggested instead of the established terms beginning with *man-*), but it also found a place in dictionaries. *The Official Politically Correct Dictionary and Handbook* (1993) includes:

> **differently evolved** an adjective appropriate for describing a non-human animal, particularly one who has behaved in a manner upsetting to unenlightened humans. Example: That shark isn't vicious. He/she just happens to be differently evolved.

> **follicularly challenged** bald. Also: differently hirsute; hair disadvantaged.

A combination of misdefinition and word invention is found in an online dictionary of legal terms (www. power-of-attorneys.com) where standard English words and phrases are deliberately misinterpreted:

> **appeal** something a person slips on in a grocery store and which results in a lawsuit being filed against said store

> **pro bono** lawyers who prefer Sonny over Cher

Where there is no relationship at all between the comic and the usual meaning, and where the context gives no clues, this type of definition becomes a test of mental agility. These puns are from the online *Humorous Dictionary*:

> **avoidable** what a bullfighter tries to do

> **subdued** a guy that works on submarines

A similar example of the playful use of the definition format can be found in the long-running Radio 4 show *I'm Sorry, I Haven't a Clue*. In the 'Uxbridge English Dictionary' round, panellists are invited to supply frivolous definitions of words, usually – as is appropriate for the medium of radio – involving a play on the sound of the word. Hence:

arcane Liverpudlian bamboo

aromatic a handy gadget used by Robin Hood

Although dictionaries can be used for many purposes, from checking spelling or pronunciation to settling a dispute, their main function is to explain the meaning of words. It's hard to make the absence of a definition amusing, but in 1927–8 *The Columbia Jester*, a student newspaper, managed it in four instalments of an 'Unabridged Collegiate Dictionary':

dress you can see through this yourself!

matrimony speak now or forever hold your peace

night gown hey hey!

Looking back at the English of the previous century in his *Passing English of the Victorian Era*, James Redding Ware in 1909 also avoided defining terms which in his case he considered too offensive to explain:

part that goes over the fence last (*American*) evident

propers (*Low. Class*) Meaning refused – but thoroughly comprehended by the coster classes. Erotic.

Ware wasn't alone in refusing or being unable to define terms listed in his dictionary:

> **bagpipe, to bagpipe** a lascivious practice too indecent for explanation.
>
> Grose, *Classical Dictionary of the Vulgar Tongue*

> **FIFO** Fit In or *Foxtrot Oscar: 'Look, mate – in this little outfit you've got to FIFO – see?' …
>
> Jolly, *Jackspeak*

> **rouge** a football term, used to express an advantage gained by one side over the other. It is obtained by touching the ball where it lies behind the enemy's quarters. It may eventually lead to a goal, but the rules are too complicated for me to explain.
>
> Nugent-Bankes, *A Day of My Life*

George Nugent-Bankes was a schoolboy at Eton when he wrote an account of a single day's events. He included a glossary as an afterthought, complaining that it was harder to write than the rest of the book put together. His refusal to explain the rules of Eton football is in keeping with the character of the narrator, who does as little work as necessary and is more interested in his social and sporting life than education.

In *Jackspeak*, Jolly, who describes himself as 'a Surgeon Commander in the Royal Navy', draws his readers into complicity in an obscene usage by failing to define it. The cross-reference sends them to a definition of *Foxtrot Oscar* that reads 'The classic, phonetically-expressed invitation to investigate *sex* and *travel*'. A reader who didn't anticipate this meaning might enjoy the surprise; a reader who did would enjoy a sense of community with other initiates. No one is likely to be offended, because nothing obscene has been said.

Grose, in his *Classical Dictionary of the Vulgar Tongue*, draws attention to his obscenities by loudly refusing to define them – he could have just left them out. Until relatively recently most dictionaries did choose quiet omission as the best way to deal with offensive words. Guy Miège took the curious step in his *Great French Dictionary* of noting, towards the end of the letter 'F', that he had omitted a commonly used term.

Of course it goes without saying that anyone who's ever thumbed through a dictionary in a boring English lesson knows just how hilarious rude words can become, even (or especially) when they are quite plainly defined.

So far we have concentrated on the headword and definition parts of a dictionary entry. These are the most obvious targets for comic lexicographers, but by no means the only ones. Etymologies can be written in a style often bordering on the incomprehensible. This makes it possible to insert absurd etymologies in the hope that the reader will foolishly believe them to be true. An article called 'Army Terms and Their Derivation' in the *B.E.F. Times* (1917), offers:

> **camouflage** from *camel* and *flag*, referring to the device adopted by this animal of tying a flag to its tail, and thus disguising itself as a ship of the desert. Hence – to deceive.

Gideon Wurdz's *Foolish Dictionary* (1904) includes several comic etymologies:

> **cajole** from Grk. *kalos*, beautiful, and Eng. *jolly*, to jolly beautifully

> **jockey** from *jog*, to move slowly, and *key*, something that makes fast. Hence, one who makes the pace fast or slow, according to instructions

The cross-reference is another unlikely source of dictionary humour. Comic cross-references in Banks's *Unabridged Collegiate Dictionary* include:

> **burlesque** see *undraped*

> **cash** see *Papa*

> **easy** see *speak*

Anyone daft enough to follow the cross-references would find no entry for *undraped*, *Papa*, or *speak*. Frederic Mullally's *The Penthouse Sexicon* (1968) sometimes does provide an entry for the user who actually follows up the cross-reference:

amulet anything carried about the person as an imagined preservative against bad luck. See *diaphragm*.

Egyptologist one who digs older women. See *mummy's boy*.

– but they rarely offer any help. In each case, the puzzled dictionary-user is more likely to understand the entry by stopping and thinking.

Some dictionaries don't expect their readers to take anything on trust. If they say that a word is used with a certain meaning, they'll prove it with an example or *citation*. They'll give an example (or sometimes lots of examples) of each word being used with that particular meaning, and what's more, they'll tell you who used it, when, and where. So if you don't believe them, you can check it out. That's why the *Oxford English Dictionary* is so very big. Concise dictionaries sometimes just give a name (e.g. 'Shakespeare') or a title ('Pickwick Papers').

The citation can occasionally supply extra humour in the dictionary format. Bestselling *Roger's Profanisaurus*, a humorous and extremely rude dictionary which is an offshoot of *Viz* magazine, sometimes illustrates its entries with completely invented citations. For instance:

salad dodger
A contumelious epithet for a fat bastard. One who at a buffet sidesteps the lettuce and celery and heads straight for the pork pies. 'Contrarywise', continued Tweedledee, 'if it was so, it might be; and if it were so, it would be; but as it isn't, it ain't. That's logic.' 'That's not logic, that's bollocks, you salad dodger.' (from *Through the Looking Glass* by Lewis Carroll).

It hardly needs saying that the *Profanisaurus*, subtitled 'The World's Sweariest Dictionary', also subverts the convention that definitions should be written in a formal style and should be suitable for any audience.

Some dictionaries provide diagrams and pictures to

explain or illustrate the meaning of words. Typically this might be a stylized line-drawing of a flower with an arrow pointing to the stamen, or a picture of two closely related animals side by side to make it easier to distinguish between them. Illustrations in this style appear in the *Uxbridge English Dictionary*, an off-shoot of *I'm Sorry I Haven't a Clue* mentioned above. It is liveried in imitation of more serious reference works and includes humorous misdefinitions of real words. We have already seen plenty of examples of misdefinition, but in this book the illustrations present an additional level of challenge to any reader who sees the drawing before the definition. For instance, a picture of a computer-driven artificial leg is captioned 'Ipswich'. Reference to the alphabetical listing provides the definition 'What you turn your hip on with'.

Lots of slang dictionaries include cartoons. In rhyming slang dictionaries they often try to combine the rhyming slang term with its standard English meaning. You can imagine for yourself the illustrations for *dog and bone* 'telephone', *plates of meat* 'feet', and *loaf of bread* 'head'. Australian slang dictionaries are full of drunken kangaroos wearing Akubra-style hats hung with corks. Hunt and Pringle's *Service Slang* (1943), a dictionary of British World War II slang, also uses illustrations for humour. The entry for *on a peg* ('on a charge') is illustrated by a cartoon of a private hung up by his shirt collar while listening to extracts from the King's Regulations. In the cartoon for *gone for a Burton* ('missing in action'), a bored-looking St Peter is standing behind a bar, floating on a cloud. An RAF pilot with angel wings is buying a pint and re-telling the story of his last flight.

27

Dictionary humour isn't confined to dictionaries. Anything solemn, authoritative, and bound by rules is a great target for parody, and dictionaries fit the bill perfectly. They regularly feature in cartoons, for instance. From www.cartoonstock.com, Dan Reynolds has a hen looking through a dictionary and exclaiming delightedly 'I knew it! Chicken comes first!' In Craig Gillespie's cartoon 'Caveman Dictionaries', the dictionary reads:

> **Agg** ... Agg
>
> **Arg** ... Arg
>
> **Nngh** ... Nngh

My final example of dictionary humour is found in an episode of *The Simpsons* called 'Homer Defined'. In it, Homer is fêted for averting a nuclear catastrophe, and his successes and failures are documented throughout the episode by reference to a dictionary that presents his picture under relevant entries. They all follow a similar format:

> **stupid** \adj\ [L *stupidus*]
>
> 1. slow of mind
>
> 2. unintelligent
>
> 3. Homer Simpson

> **lucky** \adj\
>
> 1. prone to good fortune
>
> 2. succeeding through chance
>
> 3. Homer Simpson

fraud \noun\

1. imposter
2. fake
3. Homer Simpson

In this case the apparently comic etymology for *stupid* is actually correct. In addition to the obvious humour, there is comedy in the similarity of definitions 1 and 2 for each entry. These mock the fine distinctions in meaning and use made by lexicographers which are sometimes hard for normal people to comprehend even when patiently explained.

With any luck it is now beyond question that dictionaries really are funny (or at least, they can be). They are funny in the same way that schoolteachers, organized religion and the monarchy are funny. If they take themselves too seriously, the irreverent suffer from an irresistible urge to giggle. It's easier to surprise someone into laughter if they think they know what is coming, and the dictionary format is easily recognizable: it sets up expectations which can then be undercut.

Although the humour is occasionally less than light-hearted, the dictionary is usually the medium rather than the target. We still trust 'the dictionary'.

Now read on and enjoy ...

SOME HUMOROUS CHAMBERS DEFINITIONS

Humorous definitions have featured in *The Chambers Dictionary* ever since it was first published in 1901. Many have stood the test of time, and like *sea serpent* are still to be found unchanged in the current edition. Some have been modified over the years to fit in with the mood of the times, while others, like *vamp*, made but a very brief appearance.

Here, then, is a selection of the humorous definitions of which we are most proud, with a note of the edition of *The Chambers Dictionary* in which they first appeared.

see japanese cedar

abloom
in a blooming state
1901 edition

Agapemone
a religious community of men and women
whose 'spiritual marriages' were in some cases
not strictly spiritual
1952 edition

Ainu
a people of Japan whose abundant body hair
has been the subject of remark
1988 edition

alveary
a hive of industry, hence a dictionary
1952 edition

a priori
the term applied to reasoning ... from
pre-existing knowledge, or even cherished
prejudices
1901 edition

arm candy

someone who is invited as a partner to a
social event more to add to the glamour of
the occasion than for his or her sparkling
conversational skills
  2006 edition

ASBO

a court order that places social restrictions on
people with restricted social skills
  2006 edition

baby-sitter

one who mounts guard over a baby to relieve
the usual attendant
  1952 edition

bachelor's wife

an ideal woman with
none of the shortcomings
of married men's wives
  1952 edition

back-seat driver

someone free of
responsibility but full of
advice
  supplement to 1952 edition

see combover

33

bafflegab

the professional logorrhoea of many politicians,
officials and salespeople, characterized by prolix
abstract circumlocution and/or a profusion of
abstruse technical terminology, used as a means
of persuasion, pacification or obfuscation
1988 edition

be left holding the baby

to be left in the lurch with an irksome
responsibility
1993 edition

beady eye

used to suggest distrustful attentiveness to
another's behaviour
1993 edition

behind someone's back

without someone knowing (when they might
feel entitled to know)
1972 edition

bikini

a brief swimming costume for women, in
two separate parts; (usually plural) a pair of
scantily cut briefs, esp for women
  [From *Bikini*, an atoll of the Marshall Islands,
  scene of atom-bomb experiments in the late 1940s;

the bikini's effects on men were reputed to be
similar]
1993 edition

boy band
a pop group, targeting mainly the teenage
market, composed of young males chosen
because they look good and can dance and
sometimes even sing
2003 edition

brains trust
a number of reputedly well-informed persons
chosen to answer questions of general interest
in public and without preparation
1952 edition

buckwheat
a plant (*Polygonum* or *Fagopyrum*), its seed
used especially in Europe for feeding horses,
cattle and poultry, in America for making into
cakes for the breakfast table
1952 edition

bunkum
bombastic speechmaking intended for
newspapers rather than to persuade the
audience
1901 edition

channel-surf
to switch rapidly between different television
channels in a forlorn attempt to find anything
of interest
  2003 edition

charity begins at home
usually an excuse for not allowing it to get
abroad
  1901 edition

chav
a boorish uneducated person who appears to
have access to money but not to taste
  2006 edition

see comfort food

comb out
to search thoroughly for and remove (eg lice, men for military service)
1952 edition

combover
a vain attempt to make the most of one's dwindling resources of hair
2003 edition

comfort food
mood-enhancing food that meets the approval of one's taste buds but not of one's doctor
2008 edition

devil-dodger
someone who attends churches of various kinds, to be on the safe side
1952 edition

double-locked
locked by two turns of the key, as in some locks and many novels
1901 edition

duvet day

a day's absence from work arranged at short notice between an employee devoid of inspiration for a plausible excuse and an employer who has heard them all before
2008 edition

éclair

a cake, long in shape but short in duration, with cream filling and usually chocolate icing
1952 edition

ego, massage someone's

to flatter someone, rub someone up the right way
1993 edition

emerods
haemorrhoids; representations of them in
gold, used as charms
  1972 edition

end-reader
one who peeps at the end of a novel to see if
she got him
  1952 edition

fan dance
a solo dance in the nude (or nearly so) in
which the performer attempts concealment
(or nearly so) by tantalizing manipulation of a
fan or fans or a bunch of ostrich, etc feathers
  1972 edition

fish
to catch or try to catch or obtain fish, or
anything that may be likened to a fish
(such as seals, sponges, coral, compliments,
information or husbands)
  1952 edition

flag day
a day on which collectors solicit contributions to
a charity in exchange for small flags as badges to
secure immunity for the rest of the day
  supplement to 1901 edition

gerund-grinder
a pedantic teacher
1952 edition

ghost word
a word that has originated in the blunder of a
scribe or printer – common in dictionaries
1952 edition

grammaticaster
a piddling grammarian
1901 edition

grand concert
one that need not be taken too seriously
1952 edition

hag-weed
the common broom-plant (a broomstick being
a witch's usual aircraft)
1952 edition

handkerchief, throw the
to summon to pursuit, call upon to take one's
turn – as in children's games and royal harems
1952 edition

Havana cigar
a fine quality of cigar, fondly supposed to be
made at Havana
1952 edition

he-man
a man of exaggerated or extreme virility, or
what some women consider to be virility
1952 edition

hike
a walking tour or outing, especially of the self-
conscious kind
1952 edition

illustration
a picture or diagram elucidating, or at least
accompanying, letterpress
1952 edition

isabel
dingy yellowish grey or drab
[Origin unknown: too early in use to be from
Isabella, daughter of Philip II, who did not change
her linen for three years until Ostend was taken;
an etymological connection with Isabella of
Castile, to whom a similar legend is ascribed, is
chronologically possible but by no means certain]
1993 edition

41

jacquard loom
a loom with jacquard, which produces jacquard
1993 edition

Japanese cedar
a very tall Japanese conifer (*Cryptomeria japonica*) often dwarfed by Japanese gardeners
1952 edition

jaywalker
a careless pedestrian whom motorists are expected to avoid running down
1952 edition

kazoo
a would-be musical instrument
1988 edition

knick-knack
a small, trifling, ornamental or would-be
ornamental article
1952 edition

lady-killer
a man who is, or fancies himself, irresistible to
women
1972 edition

lead out
to conduct to execution or a dance
1952 edition

lint
small pieces of thread, fluff, etc that cling to
clothes and furniture and accumulate in the
filters of washing machines and driers and in
navels
2003 edition

live
a fishmonger's word for very fresh
supplement to 1952 edition

lunch
a restaurateur's name for an ordinary man's
dinner
1952 edition

macrology
much talk with little to say
1901 edition

madame
prefixed instead of Mrs to a French or other
foreign woman's name; used also of palmists,
milliners and musicians
1952 edition

mallemaroking
carousing of seamen in icebound ships
1972 edition

man-eater
a woman given to chasing, catching and
devouring men
1988 edition

see live

mention, not to
to say nothing of, a parenthetical rhetorical
pretence of refraining from saying all one
might say (and is about to say)
1993 edition

middle age
between youth and old age, variously reckoned
to suit the reckoner
1952 edition

misrepresent
to be an unrepresentative representative of
1952 edition

mullet
a hairstyle that is short at the
front, long at the back, and
ridiculous all round
2003 edition

nerd
a clumsy, foolish, socially inept, feeble,
unathletic, irritating or unprepossessing
person, although often (eg in computers)
knowledgeable
1998 edition

nineteen to the dozen
(of speaking, done) in great quantity, not
necessarily with equal quality
1993 edition

noose
a loop with running knot which draws tighter
the more it is pulled, used for trapping or
killing by hanging; a snare or bond generally,
especially marriage
1952 edition

odour of sanctity
a fragrance after death alleged to be evidence
of saintship; facetiously applied to the living
who have denied themselves the sensual
indulgence of washing
1952 edition

old girl
an amicably disrespectful mode of address or
reference to a female of any age or species
2003 edition

opinion
what seems to one to be probably true
1952 edition

overbridge

a bridge providing a superior crossing
2003 edition

ozone

an imagined constituent in the air of any place
that one wishes to commend
1952 edition

panda eyes

dark-ringed eyes, acquired through excessive
amounts of make-up or insufficient amounts
of sleep
2008 edition

panic room

a secure room within a building, designed as
a refuge from threats such as severe weather,
nuclear attack or disgruntled employees
2008 edition

pantagamy
a word that ought to mean universal bachelorhood, applied with unconscious irony to the universal marriage of the Perfectionists, in which every man in the community is the husband of every woman
1952 edition

peat-reek
the smoke of peat, believed by some to add a special flavour to whisky
1993 edition

perpetrate
to commit or execute (especially an offence, a poem, or a pun)
1952 edition

petting party
a gathering for the purpose of amorous caressing as an organized sport
1972 edition

Pict
(in Scottish folklore) one of a dwarfish race of underground dwellers, to whom (with the Romans, the Druids and Cromwell) ancient monuments are generally attributed
1952 edition

picture restorer
one who cleans and
restores and sometimes
ruins old pictures
1952 edition

pigeon's milk
an imaginary liquid for which
children are sent, eg on 1 April
1952 edition

pink
a person who is something of a
socialist but hardly a red
1952 edition

platinum parachute
a payment, even more extravagant than a
golden parachute, offered to a senior member
of a firm on his or her dismissal in order to
soften the fall back down to the real world
2008 edition

pock-pudding
a Scottish contemptuous name for a mere
Englishman
1952 edition

pollyanna
someone whose naive optimism may verge on
the insufferable
1993 edition

prig down
to seek to beat down (a price or the seller)
1952 edition

regift
to give (an unwanted present) as a gift to
another person, in a process which is likely to
continue almost indefinitely
2008 edition

restoration

renovations and reconstruction (sometimes
little differing from destruction) of a building,
painting, etc
  1952 edition

road hog

a swinishly selfish or boorishly reckless
motorist or other user of the road
  1952 edition

rock-salmon

dogfish or wolf-fish when being sold as food
fish
  1993 edition

rosbif

a contemptuous term applied by the French to
any person who has the misfortune to be British
2008 edition

run high

(of rivers or feelings) to be close to overflowing
2003 edition

Runyonesque

in the style of the American writer A Damon
Runyon (1884–1946), portrayer of gangsters in
their milder moments
1952 edition

Ruritania

a fictitious land of historical romance (in SE
Europe) discovered by Antony Hope
supplement to 1901 edition

Santa Claus

an improbable source of improbable benefits
1972 edition

scowl

to contract the brows in a look of baleful
malevolence
1952 edition

scrum

(rugby) a closing-in of rival forwards round the ball on the ground, or in readiness for its being inserted (by the scrum-half) between the two compact pushing masses
   1952 edition

sea serpent

an enormous marine animal of serpent-like form frequently seen and described by credulous sailors, imaginative landsmen and common liars
   1901 edition

second sight

a gift of prophetic vision attributed to certain people, especially Scottish Highlanders
   1952 edition

she-oak

an evergreen tree of the genus *Casuarina*, adapted for dry conditions
   [she, in the sense of inferior, and oak, from its grain]
   1952 edition

shiver my timbers

a stock nautical exclamation uttered by stage
sailors, etc
  1993 edition

ski mask

a knitted covering for the whole head except
the eyes, worn for protection by skiers and
bank robbers
  2008 edition

smoking concert

a concert at which smoking (euphemistically)
is allowed
  1952 edition

spatangoid

a heart urchin, a member of the Spatangoidea,
an order of more or less heart-shaped sea
urchins with eccentric anus
  1952 edition

— *see* shiver my timbers

squillion
an indefinite but definitely large number
2003 edition

Sunday saint
someone whose religion or morality is confined to Sundays
1901 edition

table, under the
not above board, illicit
1993 edition

table-turning
movements of tables (or other objects) attributed by spiritualists to the agency of spirits, and by the sceptical to collective involuntary muscular action
1901 edition

taghairm
(in the Scottish Highlands) divination; especially inspiration sought by lying in a bullock's hide behind a waterfall
1952 edition

see tracksuit

temperance hotel
one which professes to supply no alcoholic
liquors
  1988 edition

tityre-tu
a member of a 17th-century fraternity of
aristocratic hooligans
  1952 edition

tracksuit
a loose warm suit intended to be worn by
athletes when warming up or training, but
sometimes worn by others in an error of
judgement
  2003 edition

tweenager
a child who, although not yet a teenager, has
already developed an interest in pop music,
fashion and exasperating his or her parents
  2003 edition

vamp
a featherless bird of prey
  supplement to 1901 edition

waistline
a line thought of as marking the waist, but not
fixed by anatomy in women's fashions
1952 edition

wardrobe malfunction
the temporary failure of an item of clothing
to cover a part of the body that it would be
advisable to keep covered
2008 edition

welwitschia
a plant of a SW African genus (*Welwitschia*) of
one species, belonging to the Gnetaceae, with
one pair of leaves that grow indefinitely
1952 edition

xylophagan
one of the *Xylophaga*, a genus of boring
bivalves
1901 edition

yahoo
an exuberant attempt to hit the ball hard,
often with disappointing results
2003 edition

yoof
(especially of magazines, TV or radio programmes, etc) relating to, specifically aimed at, pandering to, or dealing with topics (thought to be) of interest to modern youth
1993 edition

zelatrix
a nun whose duty is to keep watch on the behaviour of the younger nuns in the convent, or on that of the mother superior
1993 edition

SOME NOTABLE DEFINITIONS

Samuel Johnson and Ambrose Bierce are justly celebrated for their witty definitions, but you don't have to be engaged in writing dictionaries to produce a memorably funny definition of a word. Some of our most famous writers, thinkers and wits have been credited with devising sharp and memorable definitions. Other definitions, often those which have caught the imagination of the public and become proverbial, have been changed and misattributed so many times over the years that their true origins have been lost.

Here follows a selection of some of our favourite notable and quotable definitions.

see camel

ability
what will get you to the top if the boss has no children
anonymous

acquaintance
a person whom we know well enough to borrow from, but not well enough to lend to
Ambrose Bierce

advertising
the science of arresting human intelligence long enough to get money from it
Stephen Leacock

alcoholic
a man who drinks more than his own doctor
quoted by Alvan Barach

alcoholic
someone you don't like who drinks as much as you
attributed to Dylan Thomas

ambassador
an honest man sent to lie abroad for the good of his country
Sir Henry Wotton

appeaser
someone who feeds a crocodile, hoping it will
eat him last
  Sir Winston Churchill

atheist
a man who has no invisible means of support
  John Buchan

bank
a place that will lend you money if you can
prove that you don't need it
  Bob Hope

banker
a fellow who lends you his umbrella when the
sun is shining and wants it back the minute it
begins to rain
  Mark Twain

bore
a person who talks when you wish him to listen
  Ambrose Bierce

boredom
perhaps the world's second worst crime. The
first is being a bore.
  Cecil Beaton

boss

someone who is early when you are late and
late when you are early
anonymous

camel

a horse designed by a committee
anonymous

Mark 1
Approved
Design
☑

celebrity

a person who works hard all his life to become
well known, then wears dark glasses to avoid
being recognized
Fred Allen

chicken
an animal you eat before it is born and after it
is dead
  anonymous

childhood
what we spend the rest of our lives overcoming
  Amy Bennett

chutzpah
that quality which enables a man who has
murdered his mother and father to throw
himself on the mercy of the court as an orphan
  Oscar Levant

classic
something that everybody wants
to have read and nobody wants to
read
  Mark Twain

coloratura soprano
a singer who has great trouble
finding the proper note, but who has
a wild time hunting for it
  anonymous

see classic

65

comfort
a state of mind produced by contemplation of
a neighbour's uneasiness
Ambrose Bierce

committee
a group of the unwilling, picked from the
unfit, to do the unnecessary
Richard Harkness

committee
a group of people who take minutes and waste
hours
anonymous

compromise
an agreement whereby
both parties get what
neither of them wanted
anonymous

see coloratura soprano

conclusion
the place where you got tired of thinking
  attributed to Arthur McBride Bloch

contraception
something to be used on every conceivable
occasion
  Spike Milligan

courtesy
the art of yawning with your mouth closed
  anonymous

critic
a man who knows the way but can't drive the
car
  Kenneth Tynan

cynic
a man who knows the price of everything and
the value of nothing
  Oscar Wilde

destiny
a tyrant's authority for crime and a fool's
excuse for failure
  Ambrose Bierce

drama

life with the dull bits taken out
Sir Alfred Hitchcock

drummer

someone who hangs around with musicians
anonymous

education

the process of casting false pearls before real swine
Irwin Edman

egotist

a person of low taste, more interested in himself than me
Ambrose Bierce

experience

the name everyone gives to their mistakes
Oscar Wilde

expert

a person who has made all the mistakes that can be made in a very narrow field
Niels Bohr

expert
someone who tells you a simple thing in a
confused way in such a fashion as to make you
think the confusion is your own fault
  William Castle

fanatic
someone who can't change their mind, and
won't change the subject
  anonymous

farmer
a man outstanding in his own field
  anonymous

fishing
a stick and a string, with a worm at one end
and a fool at the other
  Samuel Johnson

foxhunting
the unspeakable in full pursuit of the
uneatable
  Oscar Wilde

gallantry
to carry out an unselfish act for selfish motives
  Elbert Hubbard

gentleman
a man who can play the bagpipes but doesn't
anonymous

gentleman
a man who can change gear in a
Hillman Imp without getting a slap
anonymous

golf
a good walk spoiled
attributed to Mark Twain

grandparents
the people who think your
children are wonderful
although they are sure you're not raising
them properly
anonymous

hangover
the wrath of grapes
anonymous

happiness
an agreeable sensation arising from
contemplating the misery of others
Ambrose Bierce

70

home
a place where teenagers go to refuel
anonymous

husband
what is left of the lover after the nerve has
been extracted
Helen Rowland

intelligence
like a four-wheel drive, it allows you to get
stuck in more remote places.
Garrison Keillor

kiss
a lovely trick designed by nature to stop
speech when words become superfluous
Ingrid Bergman

lawyer
a legal gentleman who rescues your estate
from your enemies, and keeps it himself
Lord Brougham

lecturer
a person who talks in other people's sleep
anonymous

life
a fatal sexually transmitted disease
anonymous

life
what happens when you're busy making other plans
John Lennon

life insurance
a contract that keeps you poor all your life so that you can die rich
anonymous

marriage
a bribe to make a housekeeper think she's a householder
Thornton Wilder

martyrdom
the only way in which a man can become famous without ability
George Bernard Shaw

mayonnaise
one of the sauces which serve the French in place of a state religion
Ambrose Bierce

middle age
when age starts to show around your middle
Bob Hope

mistress
something between mister and mattress
anonymous

music
a complex organization of sounds that is set
down by the composer, incorrectly interpreted
by the conductor, who is ignored by the
musicians, the result of which is ignored by
the audience
anonymous

musicologist
a man who can read music but can't hear it
Sir Thomas Beecham

nudist beach
a place where men
and women can air
their differences
anonymous

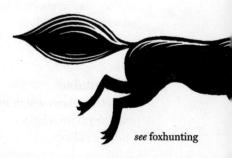

see foxhunting

oats
a grain, which in England is generally given to
horses, but in Scotland supports the people
Samuel Johnson

optimist
a person who has not had much experience
Don Marquis

originality
judicious imitation
Voltaire

overwork
a dangerous disorder affecting high public
functionaries who want to go fishing
Ambrose Bierce

 painting
the art of protecting flat surfaces from the
weather and exposing them to the critic
Ambrose Bierce

peace
in international relations, a period of cheating
between two periods of fighting
Ambrose Bierce

pessimist
a man who thinks everybody is as nasty as
himself, and hates them for it
  George Bernard Shaw

positive
mistaken at the top of one's voice
  Ambrose Bierce

psychiatrist
a man who goes to the Folies-Bergère and
looks at the audience
  Mervyn Stockwood

psychoanalysis
the cure of the id by the odd
  anonymous

see painting

puritanism
the haunting fear that someone, somewhere,
may be happy
HL Mencken

rock journalism
people who can't write interviewing people
who can't talk for people who can't read
Frank Zappa

show business
sincere insincerity
Benny Hill

song
the licensed medium for bawling, in public,
things too silly or sacred to be uttered in
ordinary speech
  Oliver Herford

spring
a season which makes you feel like whistling
even with a shoe full of slush
  Doug Larson

squirrel
a rat with good PR
  anonymous

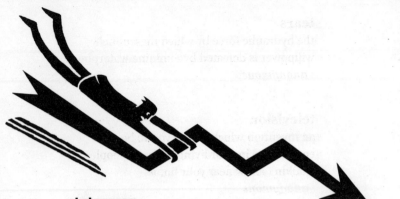

statesman
a politician who has been dead ten or
fifteen years
  Harry S Truman

see stockbroker

stockbroker
someone who invests your money until it has
all gone
  Woody Allen

tact
the ability to describe others as they see
themselves
  Abraham Lincoln

taste
a quality possessed by persons without
originality or moral courage
  George Bernard Shaw

tears
the hydraulic force by which masculine
willpower is defeated by feminine waterpower
anonymous

television
an invention which allows you to be
entertained in your living room by people you
wouldn't allow near your home
anonymous

work
the curse of the drinking classes
attributed to Oscar Wilde

year
a period of three hundred and sixty-five
disappointments
Ambrose Bierce

zeal
a nervous disorder
afflicting the young and
inexperienced
Ambrose Bierce

see television

79

THE CHAMBERS GIGGLOSSARY

Since 2003, Chambers has offered
visitors to its website the opportunity
to contribute their own humorous
definitions to *Chambers Gigglossary*.
Here is a selection of the best entries,
along with scores of brand-new
definitions of our own. We would like
to thank the many people who have
contributed to this project. If you feel
inspired to create your own amusing
definitions, why not share them with us
on our website at www.chambers.co.uk?

see
flabbergasted

A

A list
the nonesuches of the notoriocracy

abbreviation
a long word used to describe a short word
used in place of a long word

access
a process whereby the educated foist their
morality upon the uneducated

accountant
a person who will prove that two
and two did make four, but, after
deducting professional fees, now
only comes to three

analyst
a person who uncovers your emotional
poverty while causing you actual poverty

anomie
formerly, a state of instability, unease and
alienation, now renamed 'modern life'

see accountant

82

antibiotics
the ideal thing to give to the man who has everything

argument
an exchange of words between people with diametrically opposed views, all of whom know that they are right

aroma
a smell which has been to charm school

assets
liabilities waiting to happen

assumption
an error of which you are as yet unaware

astronomer
someone who is lucky enough to be paid for staring into space

autobiography
a book written about oneself, now often written by somebody else

avenue
a street with a superiority complex

bagpipes
an instrument of torture
used by the Scots against
other nations

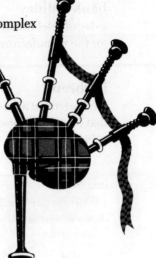

bail
an opportunity to see if you
can get away with it the
second time

bake-off
a contest won by the entrant with the most
brownie points

bald patch
something best kept under your hat

baldness
a pate worse than death

bank
an institution whose motto is 'never a
borrower or a lender be when you can be both'

bank holiday
a day of celebration and rejoicing, especially
for the manufacturers of umbrellas

barbecue
food prepared alfresco on a grill in the belief
that meat marinated in sweat and dead flies is
appetizing

barber
a man you pay to attack you with
sharp weapons

bargain
something you
didn't really want offered at a
price you can't resist

bath tap
an apparatus which water gushes
out of and big toes disappear into

see bald patch

85

batty
cricket-loving

Beelzebub
an ancient word for what we now call the
office joker

belt
a narrow strip of leather, cloth, etc, worn
around the waist to give other people the
impression that one is slim enough to require it

birthday cake
a consolation prize awarded
annually

bisexuality
an advanced form of
masochism

blogger
someone who passes each day
telling you at length that they
have nothing to tell you

blonde
a member of the fair sex

see birthday cake

blood
a liquid which sustains us, made up of red
cells, white cells, platelets, plasma and alcohol

Boat Race
an annual competition between gentlemen
and scullers

bookmaker
one who is planning to make a book named
'How to Get Rich'

bookmaker
a shopkeeper who gives place to his betters

boredom
a pig of a time

see bank holiday

87

bride
a woman with a lifetime of happiness behind her

buzzword
an irritating item of ephemera which flies in one ear, stings you, then flies out the other

cagoule
a garment designed to keep drops outside and drips inside

calcium
what chalk and cheese have in common

campanologist
a word you can't recall the meaning of, though it rings a bell

BRITISH CHEESE

capitalism
the survival of the fattest

see cheese (UK)

card
an object a magician always has up his sleeve and a salesman always has in his breast pocket

castle
formerly, the home of an
Englishman; now, the home
of a tearoom, an overpriced
giftshop and a fountain
blocked by crisp bags

cat
a partially domesticated animal who
keeps you as a pet

celery
purgatory, in vegetable form

charity
that which begins at home then stops
you every twenty yards down the
street

cheese
(UK) a delicious and nutritious
foodstuff made from the
curds of milk

cheese
(US) a foodstuff made
from the curds of milk

see cheese (US)

chihuahua
a Mexican rat which is sometimes mistaken for a dog

chin
a part of the face that
has evolved in humans
specifically to assist in
putting pillow-cases on
pillows

Christmas
a time of year when people empty their bank
accounts, come to blows with their relations
and suffer embarrassment at office parties, but
which is nevertheless referred to as a period of
rejoicing

Christmas
the season to be jolly miserable

civil list
a set of characters which cost us a fortune

civility
a characteristic which costs nothing

clanger
a bum note in a peal of bells

cliché
a tried and tested phrase which does the trick,
all things considered

cloud
a silver-lining mine

coal
black power

colloquialism
a formal word for an informal word

commemorative plate
bull*#i! in a china shop

commitment
the capacity of a would-be husband to do what
he's told

common sense
practical wisdom and understanding, and as
such, not common at all

comprehension
something that one has to get in order to get it

computer
an electronic time-saving device that is
commonly used for time-wasting activities

computer expert
someone who has not read the
instructions, but who will nevertheless
feel qualified to install a program
and, when it does not function
correctly, pronounce it incompatible
with the operating system

conductor
one who faces the music for a living

confidence
the feeling one experiences before one fully
understands the situation

consciousness
the time between one nap and the next

contract
a document that makes extortion legal

see cuckoo

co-operate
used of oneself, to enter into a constructive
collaboration with another person; used of
someone else, to do exactly as one is told

coot
a bird which shaves its head to help it to swim
faster

credit
the gift which keeps on taking

crew
a group of workers who are all in the same boat

cricket
a game with 22 players, 220 spectators and 2200 rules

cruise liner
a floating prison with better-than-average food

cuckoo
a bird which lays its eggs in other people's clocks

curiosity
a form of behaviour which used to kill cats but now mainly compels us to lick frozen poles and touch wet paint

date
an opportunity to discover why another
person is still single

daytime television
a punishment visited upon people who skive
off work

debit card
the latest invention for parting a fool and his
money

democracy
a system which ensures that everybody gets
what nobody wants

dentistry
(UK) occasional treatment
of the teeth to ensure one or
two remain in place

dentistry
(US) regular treatment
of the teeth to ensure a
perfect smile

95

desk
a semi-mythical structure believed to exist underneath all your paperwork

dieting
wishful shrinking

directions
the one thing a man will never ask a woman to give him

DIY
(abbreviation) Damage-It-Yourself

doctorate
a third degree education

see desk

96

dog
a man's best friend – after football, women,
television, beer, snooker, beer, more television,
beer...

draughtsman
one who is expected to have a chequered
career

dressing room
a workplace where mutton is transformed into
lamb

dropout
a rebel without a course

dyslexia
a medical condition whose sufferers couldn't
possibly spell it

electricity meter
a machine for counting the family joules

empathise
to identify yourself with the sort of person you
wish you were

enemy

a friend who you got to know better

English

a language that is now spoken fluently in
many countries of the world – although rarely
in England

estimate

an amount approximately equal to half of the
eventual cost

experience

the ability to repeat one's mistakes with ever-
increasing confidence

false rib

a bone of contention

falsies

an artificial
enhancement of a
young woman's bust
or an old woman's
mouth

see **estimate**

see fisherman

familiarity
a state which, though it can breed contempt, also helps us avoid having to introduce ourselves to our workmates each morning

famous
a word which is famous for being famous

fashion
a means of expressing one's individuality by wearing and doing exactly the same things as everybody else

fetishism
dirty habits recast as a minor science

financial adviser
an expert who is economical
with the truth

fisherman
one who is attempting to
disprove the old adage that
there are plenty more fish in the sea

fishmonger
a man who knows his plaice

see flabbergasted

five o'clock shadow
the dark look on the face of an office worker
with three hours overtime to be got through

flabbergasted
absolutely horrified at how much weight you
have put on

see fox

flambé
a culinary flash in the pan

flirt
to imagine the taste of more than you can chew

fool
one who announces loudly that he doesn't suffer others like him gladly

form-filling
Satan's way of ensuring we are match-fit for the afterlife below

see flambé

forty
the age at which life begins and death starts warming up on the touchline

fox
a member of the dog family which in the city is fed by elderly women and in the country is killed by elderly men

fray
a brawl which occurs when people are at a loose end

freckle
the poster boy of the blemish family

freedom of speech
the right to be listened to, given to people
in civilized societies even when they have
nothing to say

fresher
an immature student

frottage
the fine art of groping

fun
a form of enjoyment that advertising agencies
would have you believe everyone, except
yourself, is having

gaga
experiencing ultimate sentience

girlfriend
a man's future ex-wife

glamour
a term used for the beauty of the lower orders

global warming
a meteorological phenomenon cited to explain the appearance of three consecutive days of fine weather in a British summer

gobsmacked
a word only ever used by those whose gobs ought to be

goose
a bird which looks like a duck, walks like a duck and quacks like a donkey

gooseberry
a fruit you wish would leave you alone

gossip
a person who will never tell a lie if the truth will do more damage

grandmother
a creature who, when not sucking eggs, is hogging the peppermints

graphic designer
a profession which has been elevated from drawings clerk to art guru

habit
a garment which is hard to dye when it is old

handkerchief
cold storage

happiness
the stage name of delusion

heart-to-heart
a raging argument carried out in low voices

help desk
a department of a business organization that purports to combine help and a desk but invariably delivers only 50% of these

here
any place where both buck and bus rarely stop

hibernation
safety in slumbers

high court judge
someone who will try anyone once

Highway Code
a set of rules and regulations to be memorized
on the day before taking one's driving test
– and forgotten on the day after

historian
one whose future lies in the past

history
a method of recording the past to make it look
like your chaps won

holistic
describing any practice which attempts to
put a hole in the pocket of those with a hole
between their ears

home
an estate agent's word for a house

home
a place there is no place like, though Barbados
runs it close

homework

a cruel and unusual punishment, best suffered in front of the television

honesty

the best policy, unless you are after sex or money

horologist

a wind-up merchant

horrific

a word used by journalists to describe an accident on any occasion when 'tragic' is inappropriate

hospital

a place to which the sick and the injured are rushed at breakneck speed, and then asked to wait for several hours before being seen by a nurse or doctor

husband

a person who empties the waste paper bin and believes that he has cleaned the whole house

hyperbole

a cosmically elaborate and supremely convoluted figure of speech employing a literally unique amount of overstatement

hypochondria

the only illness a hypochondriac thinks he or she doesn't have

indicator board

a board displaying the time when a train or bus is scheduled to depart, as opposed to the actual departure time of the train or bus

see castle

107

innumeracy
an ineptitude for mathematics which results
in the fear of all sums

inspector
a general euphemism for what used to be
called a torturer

instruction manual
an explanation of how to use something
written in a way that is easily understood only
by the author

jalopy
a last chance saloon

January
the month of debts, darts and diets

jargon
the native tongue of any land to which you
know you never wish to travel

jeopardy
a town with an apparently high number of
unfilled jobs

jeweller
a diamond geezer who offers a silver service

jigsaw
a game designed to induce pleasure via despair

journalist
someone who knows almost nothing about almost everything

justice
a decision in your favour

keyring
a device that enables you to lose all your keys simultaneously

last orders
a daily 15 minute period generally used as a rehearsal for the end of the world

leaving party
a celebratory gathering involving a communal sigh of relief

library

a place where you will find information on every subject except the one you wanted to know about in the first place

lisp

the result of muddled lips

local council

a group of people who meet to discuss the best way of doing something before giving the job to whoever submits the cheapest tender

lodge

where a beaver is when it is not beavering away

management consultant

someone who tells you how to improve the way you do something that he or she can't do at all

manager

someone who is paid a lot of money to watch other people do all the work

manifesto
a statement of what you would get up to if you had talent, honour and principles

marketing
the art of selling a product that doesn't cost much to produce in such a way that people will take out a small loan to own it

marketing
the process whereby a spade is called a garden excavation solution

marriage
a bond formed due to a mutual lack of common sense

martial art
a technique that uses aesthetically pleasing movements to render one's opponent less aesthetically pleasing

MBA
(abbreviation) Mediocre But Ambitious

melba toast
the greatest thin singed sliced bread

menstrual cycle
a process that is repeated ova and ova again

menu
(UK) a list of many dishes to tempt you into a restaurant where you may choose from the nine dishes actually available

menu
(US) a list of many dishes which can be ordered in a restaurant

microsecond
the time it takes for your state-of-the-art computer to become obsolete

mittens
kid gloves

mobile phone
an electronic device for one-to-one communication and one-to-many irritation

Monday
the first day of the working week, usually spent calculating how many days are left until Friday

monosyllable
a contradiction in terms

mood
a unit of time used only by women, lasting approximately half an hour

morris dancer
a drinker with a dance problem

MP3 player
a device for playing music, which includes a set of earphones to ensure that it can be heard by all the other passengers on the train

mug
a cup for a person with a big mouth

mustard
a paste employed to add bad taste to worse food

mutual recursion
see: recursion, mutual

naturist
a person who prefers to go about naked, and by doing so reminds others why it is a good idea to go about clothed

navel-gazer
one who has seen the lint

neighbours
the people who live in the place that would be your back garden if only you had more money

neonate
one who wasn't born yesterday

nostril
a thing you need like a hole in the head

oil
a commodity which it is grand to have plenty of, unless you are a pilchard

oilseed rape
a crop which
grows from
tiny seeds
and massive
subsidies

orchestra
a group of musicians,
numerous but not more
than you can shake a stick at

see mittens

paranoia
why do you want to know?

partner
one's other half, who makes life twice the
trouble

party
a social gathering of people who would rather
be elsewhere

passport
a booklet in which we hide a picture of our
true self

personal trainer
a bigness consultant who specialises in waist disposal

petard
a blast from the past

phantom pregnancy
a state of labouring under a misconception

pittance
the amount a peasant is paid for removing the stones from olives

plan
1 an outline of how things are to be done, which will be completely ignored while completing the task
2 an outline of how things should have been done, drawn up after the task has been completed

poaching
the procurement of fish by hook and by crook

poet
a human sub-species, so shy they have to write
down their chat-up lines

politics
the art of answering a question with
another question

poodle
a dog breed often paraded as a
living emblem of its owner's wilful
lack of taste

postage and packing
a service for which you are
charged the price of a stamp,
an envelope and a large drink
and a cake for the person doing
the licking

pragmatist
an optimist who carries an umbrella

precision
a highly specialised form of guesswork

present
an occasion no time is like, except most of last
week and half of last month

princess
a young woman who in stories rides a unicorn
and entices heroes but in real life rides a polo
pony and attracts cads

principle
a fundamental belief which is malleable
depending on the believer's current financial
status

procrastination
a word I didn't get round to defining today but
might get round to tomorrow

promise
to state the thing which you are least likely
to do

propaganda
non-invasive brain surgery

psychiatrist
a person with a degree of mental illness

see purring

pub crawl
the shortest distance between two pints

public house
a venue where there is no smoke without fines

pug
a dog with a low profile

purring
a pleasant low sound made by cats and
engines, but not by cats in engines

pyromania
a misplaced burning ambition

quality
a meaningless word used by estate agents to add 10% to the cost of an unremarkable house

quantum leap
a tricky move in the sport of extreme trampolining

queue
other people getting in the way

quintillion
a number approximately equal to all the tea leaves in China added to all the grains of sand on a beach

rack
that upon which people do not wish to be drawn

reality
an illusion sometimes experienced by people who have not drunk enough alcohol

recommendation
a name generally used for the highest priced dish on any menu

recursion, mutual
see: mutual recursion

red nose
a plastic accessory worn at wit's end

regression
a process which enables you to lie back and relapse

revelry
the sound of people pretending to have a good time

revision
the cram before the storm

risk
an accident during its apprenticeship

sale
a period when high street stores sell goods for only twice their Internet price

savings
the end which justifies the mean

search engine
a program that enables computer users to locate information and advertisers to locate computer users

secret
something you tell to one person at a time

seethe
to quietly reflect that many are better than you at everything

short cut
a more direct route between two points, typically increasing the time it takes to reach your destination

silence
a quality which is golden, except when it is a brewing sulk

simplicity
a condition which cannot be defined on its own terms

sitcom
a type of television programme, a contraction of 'unbelievable situation' and 'absence of comedy'

skive
to work hard at not working at all

slug
a homeless snail

speed date
to shoot off after the starter when your co-diner mentions fertility or gearboxes

speed dating
an opportunity to get all your disappointments over at once

spin
the art of lying through your back teeth whilst smiling through the front ones

see slug

sport
any game devised by the English and taught to foreigners, who then promptly thrash the English at it

spouse
the person who sleeps on their own middle of the bed

sprightly
an adjective applied by journalists to anyone over the age of 60 who is still breathing

stadium
a giant structure built to contain the behaviour of overpaid sports stars and over-the-hill rock stars

statistician
a person who lacked the personality to become an accountant

sticky tape
an adhesive substance designed to stick to one finger, then another, then itself

strategists
a group of people who are getting their act together

strike
industrial inaction

stumped
to be baffled about the appeal of the game of cricket

suicide
an act that could involve jumping to a conclusion

sun
an orange-coloured heat-giving disk in the sky, described to the British by travellers from overseas

Sunday lunch
generally a headless chicken scenario

summer
a mythical British season, named from someday and rumour

superego
an advanced state of selfhood reached only by car park attendants and doctors' receptionists

surgeon
a doctor who takes you to the theatre and has you in stitches

taramasalata
a substance which some misguided souls seem truly not to mind being pink fish-egg ice cream

teacher
a person who talks to himself for a living – as opposed to a lunatic, who talks to himself for fun

technophilia
the father of invention

thermae
an early bath

thunderstorm
a rain of terror

ticket wardens
officials who have their work
down to a fine art

tideline
the extent of the tide, as marked
by driftwood, old shoes, orange
string and dead gulls

time capsule
a collection of objects gathered
to show our descendants how
tasteless and dim-witted we were

timetable
a list that sets out all the times when a
train will definitely not be departing on any
particular day

tragic
a word used by reporters to describe an
accident on any occasion when 'horrific' is
inappropriate

travel agents
the chartering classes

troubles
today's troubles are the tomorrow's troubles
you worried about yesterday

Tuesday
the second day of the working week, usually
spent wondering how it can be possible that
there are still three more days until Friday

tyrant
a politician who is no longer concealing his
ambitions and intentions

umpire
a sporting official known in cricket for crying
out loud and in tennis for not being generous
to a fault

unbelievable
a word used by sports commentators to
describe any normal event

underachiever
one who prefers to live the quite life

universal
does not fit anything properly

user guide
an incomprehensible manual written in near-English, to be opened only after trial and error has failed and/or the gadget that came with it has been broken

vagueness
a quality which it is, erm, hard to put your finger on, sort of, well, you know

veil
the part of a wedding dress which most enhances the bride's beauty

village
a community of around 200 people, half mad as fudge and half who only visit every other weekend

vindaloo

a dish which is generally consumed now and paid for later

violin

a fiddle being played by someone wearing a suit and tie

vista

a long and beautiful sun-filled view (except for viewers in Scotland)

voicemail

an automated answering service for when you are more mobile than your phone

see
washing
machine

wallet
a leather folding case that formerly contained your money but now contains your credit-card receipts

walrus
a mammal which is half sea lion, half tin-opener

washing machine
an electrical device used to turn underwear grey and shirts pink

watering hole
a soap opera for wildlife

watt
a unit of electrical power named after a man who saw his name in lights

wealth
a financial state rarely felt by the wealthy

Wednesday
the third day of the working week, usually characterized by a feeling of astonishment that it is still not yet Friday

week
a long time in politics, a much longer time in Dundee

whistling
aural torture with minimal effort

wife
a woman who has ceased to be your girlfriend and resents anyone attempting to fill the vacancy

wisdom
the ability to recognize a mistake when you make it again

woolly
a garment worn by children when their mothers feel cold

women's studies
a subject requiring broad research

wreck
a vessel which has gone down in history

wrecking ball
a device which will bring the house down

wrestling
a pantomime with added Lycra® and body odour

yawn
an honest opinion openly expressed

zombie
a fearsome creature resurrected from death or a nap after Sunday lunch

zoo
a place where you can see snakes and apes, some of whom take their children there

BIBLIOGRAPHY

Adams, Douglas, and John Lloyd, *The Meaning of Liff* (London: Pan, 1983)

'Army Terms and their Derivation', *The B.E.F. Times* 1.2, Aug. 15, 1917, pages unnumbered. Reprinted in *The B.E.F. Times* (London: Herbert Jenkins, 1918)

Bailey, Nathan, *An Universal Eymological Dictionary* (London: E. Bell and others, 1721)

Banks, J. R. McReynolds, 'An Unabridged Collegiate Dictionary', *Columbia Jester* Dec. 1927, 10; Jan. 1928, 19; Feb. 1928, 14; March 1928, 12

Beard, Henry, and Christopher Cerf's *Official Politically Correct Dictionary and Handbook* (New York: Villard Books, 1993)

Bierce, Ambrose, *The Devil's Dictionary* (1911) reprint (Mineola, NY: Dover Thrift Editions, 1993)

Blackman, John, *The Aussie Slang Dictionary for Old and New Australians* (South Melbourne: Sun Books, 1990)

Brooke-Taylor, Tim, et al., *The Uxbridge English Dictionary* (London: HarperCollins, 2005)

The Chambers Dictionary (Edinburgh: Chambers Harrap Publishers Ltd, 1901-2008)

'Definitions (in memory of H.M.F.)', *The Dump 3*, Christmas 1917, 20

'Dictionary of War Terms', *The Sling*, Oct. 1917, 39-41

'The Dictionary of War Terms', *The Listening Post 26*, July 20, 1917

Empey, Arthur Guy, *Over the Top* (London: G.P. Putnam's Sons, 1917)

Esar, Evan, *Comic Dictionary* (New York: Horizon, 1943)

The Golden Horseshoe. Written and Illustrated by Men of the 37th Division B.E.F. (London: Cassell, 1919)

Gradus ad Cantabrigiam or, a Dictionary of Terms, Academical and Colloquial, or Cant, which are used at the University of Cambridge (London: Thomas Maiden for W.J. and J. Richardson, 1803)

Grose, Francis, *Classical Dictionary of the Vulgar Tongue* (London: S. Hooper, 1785, 1788)

Hedley, Leslie Woolf, *Alphabet Soup. A Dictionary of Homo Sapiens Americanus* (Cotati, CA: EXile press, 1997)

Hunt, J. L., and A. G. Pringle, *Service Slang* (London: Faber & Faber, 1943)

Johnson, Samuel, *A Dictionary of the English Language. In which the Words are Deduced from their Originals, and Illustrated in their Different Significations by Examples from the Best Writers* (London: W. Strahan and others, 1755)

Johnston, Murray, 'Aussie Dictionary (for the use of those at home)', *Aussie. The Australian Soldiers' Magazine* (Jan. 18 1918) 10-11

Jolly, Rick and Tugg, *Jackspeak. The Pusser's Rum. Guide to Royal Navy Slanguage* (Torpoint, Cornwall: Palamanando Publishing, 1989)

Kendall, Park, *Still in the Draft* (New York: Grosset & Dunlap, 1942)

Lauder, Afferbeck, *Strine. Let Stalk Strine and Nose Tone Unturned. A Lexicon on Modern Strine Usage* (Sydney/ Auckland/London/New York: Lansdowne Press, 1965)

Maines, George, and Bruce Grant, *Wisecrack Dictionary. More than 1,000 phrases and words in every day use collected from 10,000 communications received during a newspaper prize contest and other sources – a new addition to the American dictionary* (New York: Spot News Service, 1926)

Mullally, Frederic, *The Penthouse Sexicon* (1968) reprint (London: New English Library, 1970)

Nugent-Bankes, George, *A Day of My Life; or, Every-day Experiences at Eton, by a Present Eton Boy* (New York: George R. Lockwood, 1877)

Oxford English Dictionary (Oxford: Oxford University Press, 1989)

Roger's Profanisaurus. The Magna Farta (London: Dennis, 2007)

Shaw, Frank, *Lern Yerself Scouse. How to Talk Proper in Liverpool* (1966) reprint (Liverpool: Scouse Press, 1966)

Tooné, Eruera, *Yankee Slang* (London: Harrison, 1932)

Ware, James Redding, *Passing English of the Victorian Era* (London/New York: Routledge/E.P. Dutton & Co, 1909)

Wurdz, Gideon, *Foolish Dictionary. An Exhausting Work of Reference to Un-certain English Words, their Origin, Meaning, Legitimate and Illegitimate Use, Confused by a few Pictures* (New York: Grosset & Dunlap, 1904)